Adult Coloring
Lighthouses

ZenMaster Coloring Books

Helpful Tips for Coloring

~ Sometimes the colors appear differently on paper than what you would expect. Use the color test page to play with your colors beforehand.

~ If you are using colored pencils make sure to keep them sharp. This helps when coloring smaller areas or details on the page. Fine point sharpies also work great for smaller areas.

~ Speaking of sharpies, make sure you put a scrap piece of paper behind the page you are coloring to keep the markers from bleeding to the next page.

~ When using crayons or pencils start out light. You can always go back and darken later.

~ There are so many tools for coloring: markers, sharpies, crayons, pencils, pastels, and the list goes on. Experiment with what works best for you and your designs. Though it's not necessary, using higher quality coloring utensils makes a difference.

~ If you come to a design that seems overwhelming just pick a place to start and go from there. Once you begin your creativity will quickly take over!! If you get discouraged just take a break and come back to the page later.

~ Remember to practice. Like anything else, the more you do it the better you'll get. It'll become more and more relaxing each time.

~ DON'T FOLLOW THE RULES! It's up to you how you color your designs. Just let your creativity take the lead and HAVE FUN!

COLOR TEST PAGE

COLOR TEST PAGE

Thank you for supporting
ZenMaster Coloring Books!

I aim to make sure my customers have
the most enjoyable and relaxing
coloring experience possible
and I would love to hear your
feedback!

Please leave a review on Amazon and
follow me on facebook for updates and
free coloring pages!
https://www.facebook.com/zenmastercoloringbooks/

check out more of my books at:
amazon.com/author/zenmastercoloringbooks

Free Bonus Page!
from:

Happy Summer
Coloring Book for Adults

https://amzn.com/1977939619

Also available in color by numbers!!
https://amzn.com/1986983838

And 5x8" Travel Edition!!
https://amzn.com/172614500X

Free Bonus Page!
from:

Adult Coloring Book of
Island Dreams Vacation

https://amzn.com/1976291267

Also available in color by numbers!!
https://amzn.com/1976507707

And 5x8" Travel Size!!
https://amzn.com/1796516090

Free Bonus Page!
from:

Adult Coloring Book of
Mermaids

https://amzn.com/1718920814

Also available in color by numbers!!
https://amzn.com/1718944012

And 5x8" Travel Edition!!
https://amzn.com/1726094502

BONUS PAGE! From "Zen Coloring Notebook"

Made in United States
North Haven, CT
22 January 2022

15112928R00030